Words of Wisdom

By

Sonny Thomas

ISBN: 1-4107-6513-X (e-book)
ISBN: 1-4107-6512-1 (Paperback)

This book is printed on acid free paper.

1stBooks – rev. 6/24/03

"Waiting"

Sometimes when an environment of worry is
created, time begins to stand still. It's
moments such as this that inspire our faith
and resolve.
We recognize the true value of collective
thinking and of how ever so precious time
spent with loved ones truly mean.
We should also remember that destiny awaits.

Author: Sonny Thomas

"Dreaming"

Sometimes when our special circumstances of
our well being becomes a heavy burden we
escape to our dreams to try to forget our
troubles.

Dreams are a very special part of our lives and sometimes it allows us the ability to transform our thinking from reality to a transformed state, and this makes time move faster and before you know it our ordeal is behind us.

Author: Sonny Thomas

Sometimes if we spent less time talking about what's in front of us,

and more time actually doing our work, we would not waste the time of others.

More importantly, we would get our own work done sooner without any unnecessary delays.

Sonny Thomas
December 18, 2001

PEOPLE CAN GIVE YOU A THOUSAND
REASONS AS TO WHY
SOMETHING CANNOT BE DONE.

HOWEVER WE HAVE TO CHALLENGE
OURSELVES TO BE ABLE TO GIVE ONE
REASON AS TO HOW WE CAN.

Written by: Sonny Thomas
February 1, 2001

SOMETIMES WE SPEND SO MUCH TIME
LOOKING UP FOR THE FLY BALL THAT WE
FORGET ABOUT THE "GROUND BALL" THAT
JUST SAILED UP THE MIDDLE THROUGH
OUR LEGS!

Author: Sonny Thomas
Date: 3/19/01

"VISION"

For some of us, our "vision" only extends as
fars as how a situation affects us directly.

Sonny Thomas
5/14/01

"SERENITY PRAYER"

God grant me the serenity to accept the things
I cannot change. Courage to change the
things I can, and the wisdom to know the
difference.

"INATTENTIVE"

Sometimes it's hard for some of us to come out
of the dugout. We spend so much time with

little gripes, grievances and internal squabbles; we forget that the other team is on the field scoring points.

Sonny Thomas
5/13/01

Unless we have the willingness and desire to work ourselves out of a job, we send the message that we want to keep playing and not be elevated to the "coach" of the team. Sometimes management must refrain from encouraging "want to be players" to lead when they would prefer to follow.

Sonny Thomas
5/13/01

P.S. I have been guilty of this, but I'm learned my lesson.

Sonny Thomas

Sometimes you can try so hard to help and assist others, when they can't always deal with the unfavorable news you try to alert them to. As a result, you can sometimes do more harm than good. "Silence" really is golden in certain situations.

Sonny Thomas
5/13/01

Sometimes when the team fails to take the initiative when opportunities are presented, you have to "step back" and recognize that no one wants to "lead".

Sonny Thomas
5/13/01

No one can grow if they don't reach out and accept change.

Sonny Thomas
5/13/01

"TRIVIAL PURSUIT"

Sometimes we have to recognize that we need to go outside and bring the "cavalry" in when the current team members spend more time arguing about "trivial things" instead of trying to "advance" and grow.

Does this apply to you?

Sonny Thomas
5/13/01

Sometimes we need to focus and make sense of things before we demonstrate to others we are ready to take the next step.

Sonny Thomas
5/13/01

Maturity has been something that has been absent from our current team-members, and

until we are ready to "stop shooting marbles"
we are not going "anywhere" as a group.

Sonny Thomas
5/13/01

When mistakes continue to mount and the
words "my fault" become "repetitious" we
need to "change" our game plan.

Sonny Thomas
5/13/01

When the players have to keep asking the
"coach" where is the play, we are not
coaching and we are not training/developing
our players.

Sonny Thomas
5/13/01

You have to have people on your team willing to give themselves up for the good of the team.

Dave Collins
NBC Broadcaster & Former Coach – Chicago Bulls
5/13/01

As a coach we have to train/develop our people to be successful. If people have to keep asking us what to do (what part is this, etc?) then we are not doing our job as a coach.

Sonny Thomas
5/13/01

If we want to keep doing everything ourselves, we need to re-think where it is we want to go.

Sonny Thomas
5/13/01

"ATTITUDE"

Unless we recognize that our "team-members" are not our enemies, we will never progress as an individual and/or as a team.

Sonny Thomas
5/13/01

Sometimes it's very difficult to imagine why others cannot see the real opportunities they have in order to achieve the success that waits

11

for those who are likely to reach out and "grab it". We need to be able to see past our desk to cross "success street".

Sonny Thomas
5/13/01

"EGOS"

Sometimes we have to put our sensitive egos in our "back pocket" and sit on it.

Sonny Thomas
5/13/01

"LEADER"

Sometimes when the horses are locked up in the corale, one will make every effort to break free, when others are content to stay in the corale.

What about you?

Sonny Thomas
5/13/01

"PROGRESS"

Progress favors those who study, prepare and work their plan and plan their work.

Is it in you?

Sonny Thomas
5/13/01

When mistakes happen over and over, and as a "coach" we do nothing about it. We send

the message to others that we are in the
wrong job.

Sonny Thomas
5/13/01

Sometimes unless we "alter our shot" we will
not score. Continuing to do the same thing
day in and day out without success indicates
an unwillingness to change. These types of
"bad habits" will get you an early shower.

Sonny Thomas
5/13/01

"ME"

Sometimes when we worry too much about "me" our focus gets clouded because "me" will never look out for what's good for the "team", because "me" never sees past "me".

Sonny Thomas
5/13/01

"FAILURE"

Failure is like a magnet when no one tries.

Sonny Thomas
5/13/01

Sonny Thomas

"WEAKEST LINK"

Sometimes our "weakest link" is our inability to focus, look over the mountain, and see past little trivial gripes, grievances.

> Sonny Thomas
> 5/13/01

QUOTES

It is one of the curious realities of life that otherwise sane individuals so often make mystifying, wacky, misguided, downright mind-boggling choices that they deeply regret with the passage of time.

> Doug Krikorian
> Sports Writer – Long Beach
> Press Telegram
> 5/22/01

Known as a great businessman and a distinguished gentleman, he was the type who learned the details of life. He treated the world as an open book. He was such a book of knowledge because he never stopped growing. He never stopped learning. He also was a broad thinker who often had his nose shoved in a novel, and a humanitarian.

Obituary for Former CSULB
Dean-John Parker

Note: This is my example of what many of us should emulate in our walk through our short livelihoods.

Sonny Thomas
5/23/01

"Conformity is the jailer of freedom and the enemy of growth"

Author: John F Kennedy

"The hardest jobs kids face today is learning good manners without seeing any."

Author: Fred Astaire

"Our greatest glory is not in never falling, but is rising everytime we fall."

Author: Confucius

"No man has the chance to enjoy permanent success until he begins to look in the mirror for the real cause of all his mistakes."

Author: Napoleon Hill

WORDS OF WISDOM
By Sonny Thomas – April 20, 1991

"People come and people go. Sometimes we have to take the time to get them to stop, take a look around and remember that in order to move forward people need to talk, communicate and relate.

Sometimes we never know how much others really care until we give them the opportunity to demonstrate their concerns."

"Sometimes we need to sit back and cherish the moments."

"Every now and then in life someone passes by and inspires our every emotion. We just have to make sure we follow the pattern of only the positive influences and discard the negative."

"Sometimes going through life is like a recipe. It takes a pinch of this, an ounce of that, a jigger of this, in order for our true character to really form. We just have to make sure our egos are not over-cooked."

"Sometimes the best athletes on a team can't win championships. Sometimes the tallest, strongest, biggest man loses sight of the fact that championships are won by every member of the team contributing to reach a common goal. Few have the patience to step back and let others have a chance to carry the ball. Are you guilty of this?"

"Sometimes people take so long in making a decision that is loses its impact and importance. A true leader gathers his (her) facts, consults with others and moves on, ready to face the next objective."

"Something most leaders forget is that they are only as smart as others perceive. We cannot beat our own drum and give ourselves continual credit as we are only fooling ourselves."

"The days of look at me, look what I've accomplished is gone. Most of us recognize that success by any sense or means cannot be achieved alone. No quarterback ever won a Super Bowl by blocking, tackling, passing, kicking and scoring all by himself."

"Some leaders have a hard time Handing off the ball. At some point it must be recognized that a true leader develops his people, coaches, guides and instills good principles in his people, while stepping back allowing them to shine."

"Sometimes we fail to recognize that the "art of listening" is an art form that is very precious. Very few managers practice this art. Many people who have had the best ideas are cut short/interrupted by people who feel that what they have to say is more important. Sadly, they ignore the fact that god gave us two ears to listen and only one mouth to talk. Do you think he wanted us to do more talking than listening? Think about it!!"

"Few would admit it, but it takes each of us to experience problems, confrontation, sorrow, pity, harshness, inhumanity, prejudice, favoritism, a bad boss, a lousy employee, bitching people, dishonesty, separation, a visit with the have-nots in order for us to form our true character. I just hope most of us learn how to be a better person as a result of these experiences."

"No matter how busy we are, no matter how rich some become, no matter how successful we become, no matter the achievement, one should never forget those who helped you get there. If this could be achieved then we would have more people moving forward and less who have not."

"Sometimes in life we run so fast that we fail to find out anything about the people we have met along the way. We must never forget to recognize that we can learn something from everyone we meet. Remember, everyone is better at something than we are. The true interest is to take time/patience to find out."

Very few leaders have mastered "communication" are you guilty?

Formula for Communicating a Message

1. Decide what you want to say, think about it.
2. Secure the other person's attention.
3. Transfer information clearly to the second party.
4. Get a receipt by having them repeat what they understand.
5. Acknowledge that you meant it that way.
6. Have them comment to you on their thoughts.
7. Acknowledge your understanding of their message while also getting them to agree their transmission of information was well received.

In Short

Tell someone something, get a receipt that they heard/understood what you translated and vice/versa.

Definition of a Good Manager

A good manager is like a football coach. He tries to get the best out of his people. This will require him to be very vocal with some, confrontational with others, etc. He will have to be a father figure to some, a policeman to others, a priest to some and a dragon to others. But most of all he must never forget that his success depends on the people's success and neither will go far without one another. The Trojan horse was not built by one person, nor does one person form an army.

One thing most managers forget is that people want to be treated like they are needed. If that need is acknowledged, support given, then this is the basis that makes others want to follow.

"Sometimes we tend to frown on the jobs we think are not "nothing to write home and tell mom about' such as janitor, mortician, trash truck operator, garbage men, etc. Have you stopped to consider what would happen if we had people who would not want to do their jobs?"

It really is true that "God" sometimes puts stumbling blocks in front of us for us to experience things. Sometimes we are so caught up in ourselves and things we ourselves have to do that we forget those around us. This could be considered a 'slap in the face' to get our attention so we can take note."

Positive Notes

Sometimes it takes believing in oneself in
order to achieve one's objectives.

We cannot allow excuses for not achieving
our personal goals and objectives. While it
certainly requires one getting the opportunity,
sometimes success is like a football. If you
keep running the ball the defense will "crack"
allowing you to get through.

I often looked around and saw the wealth and
riches others had, it's easy to question why
did god give others so much and those in need
very little. It took time to really recognize that
I was not forgotten.

The true measure of a person's wealth is the
gains achieved by the wealth of knowledge
received by meeting those people that

surround us. I would not trade these experiences for any amount of money.

Sometimes it takes a little bit of fear to instill in us that we have the talent to make things happen – "go for it".

Teamwork is all the weak, strong, fat, ugly, tall, insecure, non-confident, leaders, followers and losers, all pulling in the same direction forming a team to be reckoned with. With very little encouragement it (the team) will go far.

"If we could step outside of ourselves we would see our true selves, which might frighten some of us."

"Teamwork is like a marriage - you have to work at it to keep it strong and each of us must contribute."

29

"It is amazing what can happen to good ideas if we do not advertise them."

"Experience is like a professional gunslinger. Each time we achieve something, we put a "notch" on our learning capabilities."

"Sometimes we search long and hard for things that are right under our noses."

"At times we are inspired by what we see and hear. If we took the time to observe and listen then our "creative" dreams would be fulfilled."

"Imagination is a resource that we all have access to. We should never forget to cherish it."

"Sometimes our failure to remember key points places a 'gap' in our understanding."

"Sometimes we must choose our words carefully because it affects the attitude of others."

"If we treat others as we would like to be treated, everything will fall into place."

"Sometimes we have to work twice as hard to ensure we do not waste the gains that we have already made."

"Most of us react to pressure differently. Some of us can take a great deal of it, some of us stand up to much less. However, I do not like to react to pressure, I like to decide where I want to be, decide how to get there and then make it happen."

"Sometimes what motivates us more than money in our jobs is a match in values for the job we are hired to do."

"Credibility is like a shadow that will follow you throughout life. Some of us fail to recognize it at an early age."

"At times we become so engulfed in what others are doing that we fail to take care of our own problems."

"It is time for all of us to put our sensitive and insecure egos in our back pockets and get down to the business at hand which is doing our jobs."

"Sometimes we tend to hear (things) what we wish it to be."

"Sometimes God causes failure in our lives in order for us to learn how to overcome adversity."

"Some of us at times have tunnel vision. We only focus on things that have a particular interest to us as an individual."

"Unless we educate ourselves to our surroundings our collective learning capabilities will be restricted."

"In order for us to progress and grow we have to continually feed our knowledge box and devour as much reading material and on as many subjects as possible, in order to increase our learning capabilities."

"Sometimes our attitudes are based on how good our day went."

33

"We sometimes concern ourselves too much with outside problems and do not focus on what we should at present."

"Unless we develop personal goals and objectives we are left without a mission."

"We are only as smart as people allow us to be."

"Life is like a 'wishing well' unless you contribute something you can only dream."

"Success does not wait for us unless we are willing to take risks."

"Sometimes we become so set in our ways as Managers that we forget how to learn something new."

"Unless we are willing to accept criticism we will never learn how to fix anything."

"Unless we learn how to plan we will never move forward."

"Sometimes success causes some of us to become the person we thought only others could become."

"Sometimes we try too hard to find faults in others."

"Sometimes we are too quick to form opinions about others without any basis."

"Sometimes we perceive ourselves as something we are not."

Teach Me

Teach me values God, teach me love
Teach me which direction I should go
Teach me common sense God so I may share
my knowledge with others
Teach me how to treat my fellow man
Teach me how to rise above prejudice and
jealousies
But above all, teach me how to love and give
me the good common sense to know when it
is 'real'.

"Sometimes in our efforts to succeed we
unwantingly 'bruise' the egos of others.
However, we know it has to happen."

I care about others so much that:
When they fall I offer a hand to lift them up
When they cry I console them
When they are happy I rejoice with them

When they need advice I readily give it
When they dream I am there to acknowledge
that imaginative moment
When their days are 'dark' I offer 'sunshine'
When they are sad I offer hope
I treat them all as I want to be treated
I am known as 'thoughtfulness'

Give Me

Give me hope, give me courage
Give me life, give me strength and
determination
Give me light to find my way
Give me love so as I may remember gentle
moments
But most of all Lord, give me knowledge
So that I may share it with others

"God sometimes puts us in a leadership role
so as we may demonstrate our worth."

"Sometimes it is difficult for some of us to come to work and leave our egos at home."

"If we all made a commitment to share the things we have knowledge of, then there would be very few illiterate people in the world."

"Sometimes life is like a boomerang. If we throw too many rocks, they may return."

"If we dedicated our lives to controlling the things we could, and accepting the things we could not change, then we would have enough common sense to know the difference."

I am kindness, I am joy, I am happiness
You can share your innermost feelings and thoughts with me

I care about you and others
I am trustworthy, I am honest, I have integrity
I offer hope in time of despair
I offer a shoulder to cry on in times of sadness
I dispel any and all petty jealousies
What you tell me never leaves me
I offer no competition to you
I rejoice in seeing you accomplish success
I am there whenever you need me
I am called a 'friend' and God led me to you

"To be able to communicate with others is an
inspiration;
However it is frightening how some of us take
off running with words we thought we
heard."

"Sometimes people become very defensive
about something they fear."

"At times some of us create little problems for others when we are jealous of their success."

"If we worry too much about how well others are progressing, we will become insecure."

"I do not consider myself smart,
I do not consider myself any better or worse
than any fellow man,
But I have been told by God that I have
something to share.
So please put your hand in mind and follow
me because there are so many others who will
want to follow you."

Hope

"No matter how bad we think things are,
We need look no further than outside the
door

To recognize that we are doing better than
most."

The Repairman

Sometimes when I am called I can't tell you
when I'll come
Sometimes when I come I can't tell you
whether I can fix something
Sometimes when I come I can't tell you if I
have the parts to fix something.
Sometimes when I come I can't tell you if I
can get parts or not.
Sometimes when I come I can't tell you how
long the repaired item will last.
Sometimes when I come I can't tell you that I
will guarantee the repair.
But all the time I can tell you what my
charges are for, I am known as the repairman,
and more times than not my charges will floor
you.

FEAR

Fear is like a bully who approached the little
kid demanding money.
Fear is like darkness at night when you are all
alone hearing strange sounds.
Fear is like a hurried shadow that passes you
by ever so quickly.
Fear is like a sudden noise that startles one
unexpectedly.
Fear is opening a door only to find no one
standing there.
But most of all fear is only what we allow it to
be.

Our actions today, determine where we will
be tomorrow.

Sonny Thomas
7/29/01

The decisions we make today, will determine how those in authority will perceive us tomorrow.

Sonny Thomas
7/29/01

We cannot let our actions abort our future.

Sonny Thomas
7/29/01

We cannot replay, record and/or correct what we did yesterday. It's important that we have a "wake up call" and make adjustments to our character today.

Sonny Thomas
7/29/01

Some of us do not realize that this is not a "marble game" and that we are "playing for keeps".

Sonny Thomas
7/29/01

Unless we can focus on our objectives full time when needed, we are not going anywhere.

Sonny Thomas
7/29/01

Some of us never recognize that the work place is nowhere to play childish games.

Sonny Thomas
7/29/01

Sometimes if we are not careful,
We will get in our own way, in our quest for success.

Sonny Thomas
11/14/01

We cannot spend every day worrying about our performance,
We must concern ourselves with the outcome.

Sonny Thomas
11/14/01

Is it in you?

"The making of a champion, the development of toughness in the clutch, clear thinking under stress, and grace under pressure hardly ever happen without first experiencing crushing defeat leading to soul searching".

Author: Michael WilBon
<u>The Washington Post 6/9/02</u>

If you look hard enough you find that there are more "bad dogs" on the block than you "imagined".

Sonny Thomas
6/27/02

We need to be worthy of "praise" and "accolades" before they are given.

Sonny Thomas

6/30/02

Sometimes we live our lives at such "warp speed" that before we know it, the "boy" in us is "gone" and we did not have time to say "goodbye".

Sonny Thomas
6/30/02

He still cared, after mastering his game as perhaps never before, he still cared about doing his best.

Author: Bob Green

Sonny Thomas

(From the book "Hang Time" Days and
Dreams with Michael Jordan)

We cannot trade our competitive values for small gains.

Sonny Thomas
6/30/02

It's important that we look at our jobs as a "mission" and not just a "position".

<u>Sonny Thomas</u>

6/30/02

We cannot allow "objections" to flat-line our "perspective".

Sonny Thomas
6/30/02

Unfortunately some of us can't change what has been "stamped" in us.

Sonny Thomas
6/30/02

We cannot allow our voices to remain silent to a wasteful environment.

Sonny Thomas
6/30/02

Sometimes we can be too quick to give away something that really isn't ours to give.

Sonny Thomas
6/30/02

When the "rooster" is out of the "hen-house", there is no structure.

Sonny Thomas
6/30/02

Quite frequently some of us have a tendency of conceding defeat and folding our tents without being challenged.

Sonny Thomas
6/30/02

Sometimes we give away the store without being asked.

Sonny Thomas
6/30/02

"Everyone knows something better than someone."

Sonny Thomas
6/20/02

"Every man stamps his value on himself. Man is made great or small by his own will."

J.C.F. Von Schiller

"We either make ourselves miserable or we make ourselves strong. The amount of work to do either is the same."

Carol Castaneda

"It takes a lot longer for some to really understand that a relationship was not meant to work. Yet others arrive at this conclusion instantaneously."

Sonny Thomas
6/20/02

"Sometimes unless we are physically stopped and have a reality check by those who count, we do not know how much pain we cause to those who truly care."

Sonny Thomas
6/20/02

"Sometimes we must fall down ourselves to truly understand the pain that others experience."

<u>Sonny Thomas</u>

6/20/02

"Some people are so abrasive that they create an unwillingness on the part of others to want to be in their company/environment".

Sonny Thomas
6/20/02

"We cannot foreclose on the value that we were put here to add."

Sonny Thomas
6/20/02

"We cannot allow fear to degrade our intellect and positive focus."

Sonny Thomas
6/20/02

"Sometimes it's incredible to note the incompetence that surrounds the Medical Profession. Unfortunately, there does not appear to be a desire or willingness for society to challenge."

Sonny Thomas
6/20/02

"Sometimes it's very hard to assess the true potential of those who work with you because of their unwillingness to stay on top of their craft and learn what is happening in the outside environment.

Sonny Thomas
6/20/02

Isn't it ironic that <u>jealousy</u> and <u>hate</u> can cross all <u>racial</u> and <u>ethnic</u> <u>boundaries</u>, but will go out of their way to <u>"hug"</u> every <u>mother's</u> <u>child.</u>

Sonny Thomas
7/15/02

IS IT IN YOU?

Sometimes when things seem to constantly go wrong, we must assume our "hockey player" mentality and "kick ass" to get things done.

Sonny Thomas

7/9/02

CHEESECAKE

We are looking for people to make things happen and "knock" doors down. This does not include "cheesecakes".

Sonny Thomas

7/8/02

At times our "minds" tell us that we can do anything "physically", but our "bodies" are "quick" to point out otherwise.

Sonny Thomas

7/7/02

55

Some of us need a clearer idea of what our "mission" is and how to carry it out.

<u>Sonny Thomas</u>

7/7/02

Sometimes we make a "vow" of who and what we want to be. However, along the way we succumb to life's temptations.

<u>Sonny Thomas</u>

7/7/02

Somewhere in the recesses of our minds we know that we must deliver favorable and unfavorable news or we will not be successful.

<u>Sonny Thomas</u>

7/7/02

Sometimes our <u>lack</u> of "verbal finesse" allows others to see behind our "closed" doors.

<u>Sonny Thomas</u>

7/6/02

Some of us go to work every day knowing that every one of our colleagues who look us in the eyes are aware that we are not wanted.

<u>Sonny Thomas</u>

7/6/02

There are those who want the ball and want to take responsibility in crucial moments. Then there are those who want someone else to handle it. You find out real "quick" which people are which.

<u>Sonny Thomas</u>

7/6/02

There are rewards for working hard and working well, few receive these rewards.

<u>Sonny Thomas</u>

7/6/02

As hard as you try, you will always be "you".

<u>Sonny Thomas</u>

7/6/02

A man finds peace when he puts his heart into his work and does his best.

<u>Emerson</u>

Ability is like beauty; it can be very, very fleeting.

Former St Louis Cardinal Short Stop
Hall of Famer - Ozzie Smith

We cannot allow the attitude and action of others to "wound" our day.

Sonny Thomas
7/28/02

We cannot allow the pressures of life to "seal" our "joy".
We must use the "razor blade" of our <u>dreams</u> to dissect the <u>pressures</u> before us.

Sonny Thomas
7/28/02

We cannot allow the "wasted" efforts of others to "pickpocket" our dreams.

Sonny Thomas
7/28/02

We cannot let "the" difficult worker "sour" our spirits.

Sonny Thomas
7/28/02

Few recognize that failure can be a "springboard" to success because once you fail; it is no longer "feared".

Sonny Thomas
7/28/02

Sometimes we "front-load" so much onto our plates that we forget the other guy.

Sonny Thomas
7/28/02

Money and riches escape most of us, but the few who have their engines full "never recognize" what the true meaning of "full' is until the boat is empty.

We must learn that the glass cannot remain full continuously.

Sonny Thomas
7/28/02

Most people at some point in life and as situations unfold will question, "why me?" But I say, thank god it's me, so we can hastily move forward to something better.

Sonny Thomas
7/28/02

If we can just take a minute to recognize that no matter how much "bad luck" we "encounter" that there is someone else who is much worse off, our capacity for recovering will hasten.

Sonny Thomas
7/28/02

Our capacity to grow, contribute and add value is only hindered by the opportunities we ourselves fail to grasp.

Sonny Thomas
7/28/02

Sometimes man doesn't recognize what he himself truly has until it is threatened.

Sonny Thomas
7/28/02

Sometimes our many toys go unnoticed until someone else wants to play with them.

Sonny Thomas
7/28/02

Possessions become meaningless when a life is threatened.

Sonny Thomas
7/28/02

90% of us at some point in time lose track of what our job and responsibilities are.

> Sonny Thomas
> 7/28/02

As you look around your company's environment, you will find a host of characters. Few recognize that winning is a habit. Unfortunately, few have the willingness, desire and determination to do what it takes to be a "winner".

> Sonny Thomas
> 7/28/02

We will never be able to grow and add value to our company with what you did "yesterday" we must continue to add "coals" to the engine every day.

> Sonny Thomas
> 7/28/02

A bad "habit" always has someone waiting to "catch" it.   Good   habits   choose   its "benefactors".

Sonny Thomas

7/28/02

Success is a result of consistent practice of winning skills and actions; there is nothing miraculous about the process.   There is no luck involved.

Amateurs hope, professionals work.

Former Boston Celtic Great

Hall of Famer - Bill Russell

Learning is a daily experience and a lifetime mission.   We work to become, not to acquire. However, most of us get sidetracked by trying to acquire before we become.   Some of us want it all before the journey begins.

Sonny Thomas

7/28/02

Team craftsmanship is akin to going from the stage where you are working by yourself on an invention, building a car or a plane, then having to apply what you have learned to the assembly line and to the strategies of the marketplace where your craftsmanship has a pay-off in terms of winning.

Former Boston Celtic Great

Hall of Famer - Bill Russell

SOMETIMES WE NEED TO DUCK, COVER AND HOLD UNTIL THE "BULLSHIT" CLEARS OUR AIRSPACE.

Author: Sonny Thomas

Date: 4/4/02

Sometimes when people tell us something our "common sense" takes a "vacation" and refuses to come back until it decides "it wants to".

Sonny Thomas

8/8/02

Sometimes in our "haste" to start our day we "neglect" the most important thing which is to "get ready", "focus" and move "forward".

<u>Sonny Thomas</u>

8/13/02

Every now and then we all need a good, "swift" <u>kick in the ass</u> in order to get us started.

Sonny Thomas

8/13/02

Sometimes when the situation warrants, we need to move left, move right and get the hell out of the way and let someone else lead.

> Sonny Thomas
> 8/17/02

Some of us make the mistake of reacting to the last information we have received.

> Sonny Thomas
> 8/17/02

Every now and then we need to "<u>ignore</u>" the "<u>bullshit</u>" we hear from our advisors and make our own "<u>damn</u>" decisions.

> Sonny Thomas
> 8/17/02

How many of us know <u>what it is that</u> we want to do tomorrow?

Sonny Thomas
8/17/02

More times than not, when we are looking for our "key" people to "reach down deep, remove "stumbling blocks" and "execute", we get that "deer in the headlights" look and a "stare of emptiness".

Steve Bradbury
8/23/02

We cannot become a "starter" in the game unless we are prepared to "practice".

Sonny Thomas
8/26/02

Sometimes we run faster than we plan.

Sonny Thomas
8/25/02

Teamwork requires everyone going in the same direction. Why are you not following?

Sonny Thomas
8/25/02

Teamwork is picking up a teammate when he has fallen. Is your hand out?

Sonny Thomas
8/25/02

My greatest fear is that there is no willingness and desire to learn?

Sonny Thomas
8/25/02

Too many times there is an absence of eagerness to learn. Is this you?

> Sonny Thomas
> 8/25/02

Can you truthfully say that you will not let technology pass you by?

> Sonny Thomas
> 8/25/02

Sometimes we need to put our goddamn foot down and say "no".

> Sonny Thomas
> 8/25/02

Sometimes we let others take us out of our "game".

Sonny Thomas

8/25/02

In order to be a leader we must have the capability of delivering favorable and unfavorable news.

Sonny Thomas

8/25/02

If we are not learning something new every day, we need a set of new friends or teammates.

Sonny Thomas

8/25/02

We must progress through our jobs and leave it better than we found it.

Sonny Thomas
8/25/02

Sometimes we need to be alone to recognize that we really do have the desire and willingness to "kick ass" and get this "party started".

Sonny Thomas
8/25/02

Everyone knows something better than someone and the sad part of it is that "few" recognize it.

Sonny Thomas
8/25/02

Sometimes we can try so hard to move forward and yet every step we take it's clear that obstacles are put in place that clearly demonstrates that we are clearly not in control of our destiny.

Sonny Thomas

8/25/02

There seems to be at every turn a person who clearly demonstrates that they are not on our team.

Sonny Thomas

8/25/02

Sometimes we need to "hop", "skip" and "kick the shit" out of negativity.

Sonny Thomas

8/25/02

I often wonder how many of "you" want to devote time and attention to making "winning" a "habit".

Sonny Thomas
8/25/02

What ever happened to devotion to a desire and willingness to "successfulness"?

Sonny Thomas
8/25/02

Man delivers his best when he is pressed (under pressure).

Sonny Thomas
10/4/02

Progress has been something that we have strived to achieve for so long, and yet it still appears to be something that is imaginary when we measure our key people.

Sonny Thomas

10/7/02

More times than not, most of us fail to imagine the possibilities.

<u>Sonny Thomas</u>

10/15/02

Sometimes we spend a lot of time trying to make a "bad thing" sound "good".

<u>Sonny Thomas</u>

10/16/02

Sometimes if you stay too long at the "dance" your "character" will be "exposed".

Sonny Thomas
7/5/02

Sometimes we try so hard to make a relationship we know shouldn't work actually "work" – did it?

Sonny Thomas
7/4/02

Sometimes the observation of others is ignored and we climb on board too late.

Sonny Thomas
7/4/02

Sometimes "fear" makes the "man" in us "disappear".

> Sonny Thomas
> 7/4/02

We cannot always be the "person" others want us to "be".

> Sonny Thomas
> 7/4/02

Sometimes we travel all over the world looking for that special something only to find that it was right under our "nose" and once we recognize it, we don't want to ever leave it.

> Written for: Grandaughter, Amber Perez
> Sonny Thomas
> 7/4/02

Sonny Thomas

Sometimes love and relationships are like a "fire-fly" unless you "grab it quickly" it disappears.

Sonny Thomas

7/4/02

As we go through life, it doesn't take long for us to know "just when we have found that very special someone". More importantly, we must seize the moment.

Sonny Thomas

7/4/02

Sometimes we "run" so "fast" that we miss the "message" that others are "sending".

Sonny Thomas

7/4/02

Few of us recognize that "life" is like having "sex", if we "rush it" we don't know just how "good" it "was".

Sonny Thomas
7/4/02

Sometimes, things can be so good to us that we let our "guard" down and "miss" the very "thing" we should be more protective of.

Sonny Thomas
7/4/02

Few recognize that life is a "cycle" and we always will experience happiness, sadness and contentment. Better yet, we will not stay "parked" in this cycle for long periods of time.

Sonny Thomas
7/4/02

We really need to take the "bite" out of the "apple" for it to "taste" good.

Sonny Thomas

7/4/02

We can "fool" people for "just" so "long" before we are exposed.

<u>Sonny Thomas</u>

7/4/02

We can "throw" the "ball" over and over, but it doesn't matter unless there is someone out there who "wants" to "catch" it.

Sonny Thomas

7/4/02

Sometimes the very thing we become "tired" of becomes someone else's "commodity".

Sonny Thomas

7/4/02

"I don't know why" when others are given opportunities that they "don't" hear it "knocking".

Sonny Thomas

7/4/02

Sometimes we have a "tendency" to play so much that we don't always recognize when "it's time" to "play for keeps".

Sonny Thomas

7/4/02

One "word" can "damage" all the good things we have done in "less" than a "second".

Sonny Thomas

7/4/02

"Herding" <u>cattle</u> is a hell of a lot "easier" than trying to "lead" people over the "mountain".

Sonny Thomas

7/4/02

One minute of silence and observing what's "happening" in our surroundings will "educate" us for life.

Sonny Thomas

7/4/02

Others "perceive" us by the company we keep.

Sonny Thomas

7/4/02

Sometimes we get our "heads" bumped so much in life that we forget to put our "helmets" on.

Sonny Thomas
7/4/02

For some it takes a long time to "recognize" that others "just" don't want us "around".

Sonny Thomas
7/4/02

Sometimes "words" do more than "bruise" EGOS.

Sonny Thomas
7/4/02

Unless we "till" the "soil" nothing "grows".

Sonny Thomas
7/4/02

Sometimes we have to "hop", "skip" and "kick ass" in order to move progress to the "fore-front".

Sonny Thomas
7/4/02

Have you ever felt that so much "shit" has been "thrown" at you that at some point someone is going to say "enough is enough".

Sonny Thomas
7/4/02

No matter how much we tell people about things it, doesn't mean "shit" until they "find" out for themselves.

Sonny Thomas
7/4/02

Isn't it ironic how people can be so "critical" of something "others" do until they learn that it was their "advice" that was "acted" upon.

Sonny Thomas
7/4/02

Few people recognize that "unless" their "contributions" are recognized by others, "nothing happens".

Sonny Thomas
7/4/02

Unless we can "deliver" the mail "no one" wants to buy our "stock".

Sonny Thomas
7/4/02

Sometimes we really need to think about what we say to "others" as it just may "not" be forgotten.

Sonny Thomas

7/4/02

Every "move" we make, every "word" we say, and everything we "do" is remembered by "someone".

Sonny Thomas

7/4/02

Some of us spend so much time running away from life's problems and yet we fail to recognize that when it is all "said and done" we will never be able to "escape" until we "drive the bus".

Sonny Thomas

7/4/02

It takes most of us a long time (some of us forever) to recognize that there really is a "formula" for "everything".

Sonny Thomas
7/4/02

For every person who causes "hurt" there are "two" people who offer "help". More times than "not" they are "within" your "reach".

Sonny Thomas
7/4/02

For every problem that "confronts" us the "answer" lies within "15 feet" of us.

Sonny Thomas
7/4/02

"Shit" really does happen. However, it's what you do to get it "off you" that really "matters".

Sonny Thomas

7/4/02

Sometimes we need to "kick, punt and pass" to get where we need to "be".

<u>Sonny Thomas</u>

7/4/02

We get very few "free throws" in "life". We have to be sure that "we" make every "shot" <u>count</u>.

Sonny Thomas

7/4/02

We cannot allow what others think of us to "determine" which "choice" we make in "life".

Sonny Thomas
7/4/02

Sometimes we need to "bite off" all we can "chew" so we can be <u>all</u> that we can be.

Author: Sonny Thomas
Date: 1/20/02

Never let the show get in the way of the game.

Author: Bill Walton
Former Basketball great NBC Commentator
Date: 5/18/02

"FEAR"

Fear is a state of mind whereby many have "given up" and have the "willingness and desire" to give the ball to others because "they" themselves cannot "deliver the mail" for a number of reasons.

Author: Sonny Thomas

Date: 5/19/02

"Me"

"Me" is a person who thinks only of himself, and can never be counted on to do anything for the team.

Author: Sonny Thomas

Date: 5/19/02

The best place to find a helping hand is at the end of your arm.

Swedish Proverb

SOMETIMES WE NEVER KNOW HOW MUCH WE NEED ONE ANOTHER UNTIL ONE OF US IS GONE.

Sonny Thomas

11/22/02

LIFE

Every now and then, life will require us to "kick ass" and "move forward". Our biggest problem is that we must in our own heart of hearts recognize when it is time.

Sonny Thomas

1/8/02

LOST

The hardest part of moving forward is when no one else is ready. It's important that you recognize that you cannot get lost in that moment.

Sonny Thomas

1/8/02

BE STILL

Most of us fail to take the time to realize that we face an urgent need to be still and let life breathe its energies inside of us.

Sonny Thomas

1/8/02

FOCUS

LiFe is what we make it and no one can target where our destiny will take us. If we succumb, someone else will decide our fate.

<u>Sonny Thomas</u>

1/8/02

FEAR

Fear is a distant memory until such time as it holds our hand.

<u>Sonny Thomas</u>

1/8/02

DESTINY

We cannot allow others to decide our destiny.

Sonny Thomas

1/8/02

FEAR.COM

Some of us are so damn afraid of confronting our fears that we allow issues to overwhelm us.

Sonny Thomas

1/8/02

GOALS

Unless we dedicate ourselves to confronting hard issues, we will allow others to have an opportunity to see our true weaknesses.

Sonny Thomas

1/8/02

About the Author

Sonny Thomas has been a professional in a variety of Senior Management positions for a number of large and small companies. He has been a business turn around professional for over 25 years. He currently works for a mid-size motorcycle seat manufacturing company as Vice President.

Sonny resides in Long Beach, California with his wife Dell.